AN HACHETTE UK COMPANY
WWW.HACHETTE.CO.UK

FIRST PUBLISHED IN GREAT BRITAIN IN 2018 BY ILEX, A DIVISION OF OCTOPUS PUBLISHING GROUP LTD
CARMELITE HOUSE
50 VICTORIA EMBANKMENT
LONDON EC4Y 0DZ
WWW.OCTOPUSBOOKS.CO.UK

DISTRIBUTED IN THE US BY
HACHETTE BOOK GROUP
1290 AVENUE OF THE AMERICAS
4TH AND 5TH FLOORS
NEW YORK, NY 10104

DISTRIBUTED IN CANADA BY
CANADIAN MANDA GROUP
664 ANNETTE ST.
TORONTO, ONTARIO, CANADA M6S 2C8

EDITORIAL DIRECTOR: HELEN ROCHESTER
MANAGING EDITOR: FRANK GALLAUGHER
EDITOR: JENNY DYE
PUBLISHING ASSISTANT: STEPHANIE HETHERINGTON
ART DIRECTOR: JULIE WEIR
DESIGNER: E-DIGITAL DESIGN
PRODUCTION MANAGER: PETER HUNT

ISBN 978-1-78157-635-9

A CIP CATALOGUE RECORD FOR THIS BOOK IS AVAILABLE FROM THE BRITISH LIBRARY.

PRINTED AND BOUND IN THE CZECH REPUBLIC

10 9 8 7 6 5 4 3 2 1

#SQUAD GOALS

THE FRIENDSHIP BOOK

ELLA KASPEROWICZ

ilex

WARNING: THIS BOOK CONTAINS NUDITY, LOTS OF ALCOHOL AND LEOPARD PRINT. THE STORY, ALL CHARACTERS AND INCIDENTS PORTRAYED IN THIS BOOK ARE NOT ENTIRELY FICTITIOUS. ANY RESEMBLANCE TO ACTUAL PERSONS IS ALMOST CERTAINLY INTENTIONAL (BUT YOU KNOW WHO YOU ARE).

CONTENTS

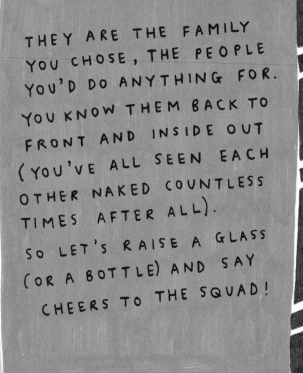

THEY ARE THE FAMILY
YOU CHOSE, THE PEOPLE
YOU'D DO ANYTHING FOR.
YOU KNOW THEM BACK TO
FRONT AND INSIDE OUT
(YOU'VE ALL SEEN EACH
OTHER NAKED COUNTLESS
TIMES AFTER ALL).

SO LET'S RAISE A GLASS
(OR A BOTTLE) AND SAY
CHEERS TO THE SQUAD!

GOOD SQUADS CONSIST OF FABULOUS INDIVIDUAL
ITEMS THAT TOGETHER MAKE AN EVEN MORE
FABULOUS CONCOCTION...

LIKE A FULL ENGLISH BREAKFAST...

OR A GIRL BAND...

OR A TOP OUTFIT...

OR TOM HARDY'S BODY.

9

WHAT SQUAD ARE YOU MOST LIKE?

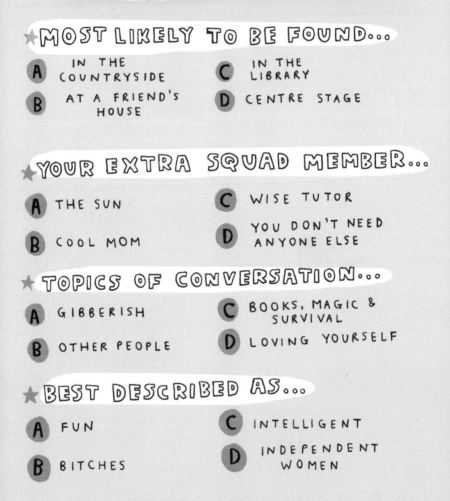

★ MOST LIKELY TO BE FOUND...

- A IN THE COUNTRYSIDE
- B AT A FRIEND'S HOUSE
- C IN THE LIBRARY
- D CENTRE STAGE

★ YOUR EXTRA SQUAD MEMBER...

- A THE SUN
- B COOL MOM
- C WISE TUTOR
- D YOU DON'T NEED ANYONE ELSE

★ TOPICS OF CONVERSATION...

- A GIBBERISH
- B OTHER PEOPLE
- C BOOKS, MAGIC & SURVIVAL
- D LOVING YOURSELF

★ BEST DESCRIBED AS...

- A FUN
- B BITCHES
- C INTELLIGENT
- D INDEPENDENT WOMEN

YOUR GROUP PET WOULD BE...

A A RABBIT

B A HANDBAG DOG

C A SNOWY OWL

D LEOPARD PRINT (totally counts)

MOST LIKELY TO WEAR...

A BRIGHT COLOURS

B PINK, LYCRA & GLITTER

C BLACK

D CROPPED TOPS, CAMO & DOUBLE DENIM

YOU MUTUALLY HATE...

A VIOLENCE

B SWEATPANTS

C MONSTERS FROM THE PAST

D BAD BOYS

WHICH QUOTE APPLIES TO YOU?

A WE LOVE EACH OTHER VERY MUCH

B GET IN LOSER, WE'RE GOING SHOPPING

C WE'RE WITH YOU WHATEVER HAPPENS

D ALL THE LADIES WHO TRULY FEEL ME, THROW YOUR HANDS UP AT ME

MOSTLY A'S : TELETUBBIES

YOU LOVE THE OUTDOORS, HAVING FUN AND
FIGURING OUT THE ADULT WORLD TOGETHER.
(ALSO NETFLIX ON YOUR BELLY = USEFUL).

MOSTLY B'S: THE PLASTICS

YOU'RE ABSOLUTE BITCHES AND ABSOLUTELY
PERFECT FOR ONE ANOTHER. PLUS, YOU'VE GOT
EACH OTHER'S BACKS (UNLESS YOU WEAR
SWEATPANTS ON MONDAY).

MOSTLY C'S: HARRY, RON & HERMIONE

JUST LIKE THE SPICE GIRLS, THERE'S A GINGER ONE, A POSH ONE AND A SPORTY ONE (IF QUIDDITCH COUNTS). YOU'RE ALL SUPER SMART AND HELP EACH OTHER FIGHT MEN FROM THE PAST.

MOSTLY D'S: DESTINY'S CHILD

YOU'RE THE MOST BADASS SQUAD OF ALL AND YOUR ADVICE TO ONE ANOTHER AND THE WORLD IS TIMELESS (UNLIKE SOME OF THOSE NINETIES FASHION CHOICES...)

YOU'VE SEEN EACH OTHER AT YOUR VERY BEST...

15

IN FACT, YOU'VE WITNESSED PARTS OF
EACH OTHER YOU COULD HAVE LIVED WITHOUT...

17

MOST LIKELY TO...

BECOME A CRAZY CAT LADY

GO ON A CHAT
SHOW

SECRETLY BE
A PRINCESS

BECOME A ROCK STAR

BE PRESIDENT OF THE UNITED STATES

LIVE TO 100 (AND LOOK BANGIN')

WITH ANY LUCK, YOU'VE GOT YOUR WHOLE FUTURES TOGETHER TO LOOK FORWARD TO...

BUY A HOUSE

GET A DOG (PRAM OPTIONAL)

PREDICTION: _____   _____
REAL LIFE: _____   _____

TRAVEL THE WORLD

FIGURE OUT ADULTING

PREDICTION: _____   _____
REAL LIFE: _____   _____

IF YOUR CALENDAR IS THE STUFF YOU HAVE TO DO, YOUR GALENDAR IS WHAT YOU LIVE FOR. WHETHER IT'S A MID-WEEK CATCH UP, A BIG NIGHT OUT OR A DAY TRIP, THE BEHIND-THE-SCENES IS FAR MORE HILARIOUS THAN THE INSTA-WORTHY STUFF...

FESTIVAL DAY TICKET ★ ENTRY○

JANUARY

MARCH

PUSSY GRABS BACK

WE CAN WEAR WHAT WE WANT

HERE COME THE GIRLS

FOR SOMETHING IMPORTANT

MAY

5QU4D

ROAD TRIP

AUGUST

BBQ

NOVEMBER

THE 'LET'S GET SOME
FRESH AIR' WALK

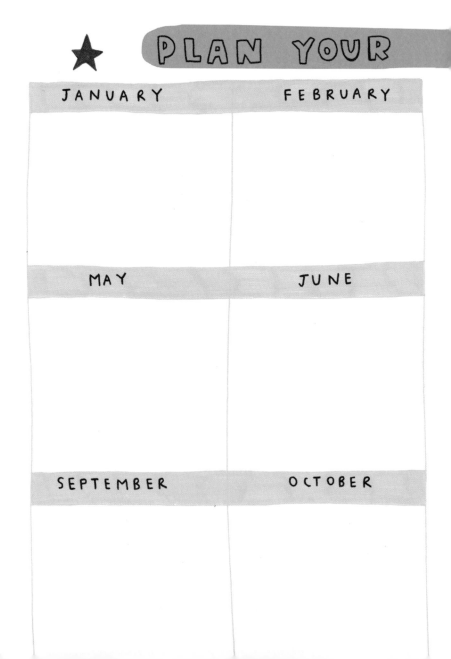

★ PLAN YOUR

JANUARY	FEBRUARY

MAY	JUNE

SEPTEMBER	OCTOBER

CALENDAR

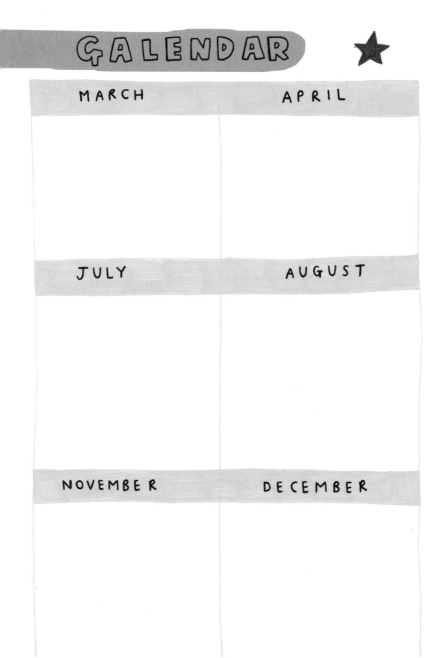

MARCH	APRIL
JULY	AUGUST
NOVEMBER	DECEMBER

CHAPTER THREE

Trending Now

SLOB GOALS

Cheese & Whine

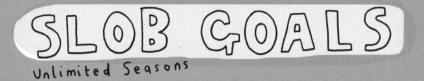

SLOB GOALS

Unlimited Seasons

HAVEN'T YOU HEARD? STAYING IN IS THE NEW GOING OUT! QUALITY TIME WITH YOUR MATES HAS NEVER BEEN SO LAZY.

Starring : THE SQUAD, FOOD, THE COOL MOM

⊕ GOALS 👍 ✍

WONDERING HOW SOME WOMEN LOOK SEXY IN DRESSING GOWNS

NOTHING ABOUT THE OUTFIT SAYS 'PARTY' OR 'WORK'

HOLE-Y JUMPER

SECRET SNACK POCKETS

DRESSING ~~BALL~~ GOWNS

CASUAL ~~SMART~~ CASUAL

46

BEST DOCUMENTARY...

BEST TV SERIES...

FEEL-GOOD FILM...

BEST TV CHANNEL...

ALL-TIME FAVE(S)...

BLAST FROM THE PAST...

RATING: ☆☆☆☆☆

Maskerade

IF YOU WERE EACH A PIZZA, WHO WOULD BE WHAT?

MARGHERITA
(PLAIN JANE)

EXTRA
HOT

PEPPERONI

HAWAIIAN

FOUR CHEESE

FIORENTINA

BBQ CHICKEN

VEGGIE

TUNA
SWEETCORN

57

OTHER (IN)ACTIVITIES

WHICH ONE'S BOY 1?

JUST ONE KISS?

PLAY IT COOL

A KISS! YOU'RE GONNA GET MARRIED

Boy 1

Hi x

WHAT DOES HE MEAN, HI?

EXCITING!

OMG

HOW LONG DO I WAIT TO REPLY?

SHIT, HE'S SEEN THAT YOU'VE READ IT

DISSECTING TEXTS

SYNCHRONIZED PERIOD DAY

LEARN A CRAFT

WITCHCRAFT

THIS CHAPTER IS A CELEBRATION
OF THE HOLY GROUP CHAT, A
WAY OF RELIGIOUSLY STAYING IN
TOUCH WHEN YOU HAVE TO BE
APART. IT'S OMNISCIENT AND
OMNIPRESENT AND WHILE THE
CONSTANT BUZZING AND PINGING
ANNOYS EVERYONE AROUND YOU,
IT IS THE THEME TUNE TO YOUR
LIVES. 'OMG' REALLY IS THE NEW
'911',* AND EVERYTHING IS DISCUSSED,
FROM THE IMPORTANT TO THE
USELESS TO THE RIDICULOUS.

* IN A MEDICAL EMERGENCY,
SERIOUSLY, GET YOURSELF TO
HOSPITAL... AND THEN POST IN
THE GROUP.

I THINK I HAVE CHLAMYDIA
I'VE QUIT MY SHIT JOB!
MISS YOU ALL
IF SOMEONE GAVE YOU $100,000 TO STOP DRINKING, WOULD YOU DO IT?
I HOPE OUR KIDS HAVE THEIR OWN GROUP CHAT
EW
WE HAD SEX!
I'M SOOOOO HUNGOVER, SEND HELP
UGH
LOOK AT THIS DOG IN A CHRISTMAS JUMPER
I NEED SUN AND FUN, WHO WANTS TO GO AWAY?
HOW DO I WAX MY OWN VAGINA?
CAN YOU TYPE PROPERLY?
WOULD YOU RATHER ONLY EVER HAVE SEX LISTENING TO 2 BECOME 1 BY THE SPICE GIRLS OR ONLY EVER DRINK LISTENING TO DESPACITO?
WHY DON'T BOYS REPLY AS QUICKLY AS YOU LOT?
WHAT THE FUDGE?
I DON'T THINK MY DAD UNDERSTANDS THIS EMOJI... LOL
I'M FEELING FRAGILE

I WOULD LOOK LIKE A SAUSAGE DRESSED LIKE THAT
YOU LOOK FAB
INTERVIEW IN TEN MINS
TELL US EVERYTHING!
WE HAVE REACHED 10,000 MESSAGES!
YOU NEED A SUGAR DADDY
WHAT IS A NORMAL PORTION OF CHIPS?
WHY AREN'T WE RICH AND FAMOUS YET?
CAN YOU HAVE SEX ON YOUR PERIOD?
HOW DO I END AN EMAIL?
THIS TIME LAST YEAR WE WERE ON THE BEACH
OMG GUESS WHO JUST LIKED MY PHOTO
HOW DO I WORK LINKEDIN?
WOULD YOU RATHER SLEEP WITH CHANDLER, JOEY OR RACHEL?
WILL YOU ALL GO LIKE MY PHOTO PLEASE?
I AM A SASSY KEBAB
CAN THE DOCTOR PRESCRIBE PROSECCO?
WHY IS EVERYONE GETTING PREGNANT?
DO ITTTT
ON MY WAY!
SORRY, WHAT?
NEED A POO. THE TOILET DOESN'T HAVE A WORKING LOCK

EVOLUTION OF THE GROUP CHAT

1980s - STRANGER THINGS

WALKIE-
TALKIES
MAY BE
UNRELIABLE
BUT YOU
CAN
COMMUNICATE
WITH PEOPLE
IN OTHER
DIMENSIONS...

1990s - CLUELESS

THE BRICK
PHONES ARE
SO BIG, IT'S
A WORKOUT
CARRYING
THEM AROUND
BUT THEY
ALLOW
CONSTANT,
POINTLESS
CHATTING.

2000s - MEAN GIRLS

SORRY TO REFERENCE MEAN GIRLS AGAIN
BUT THIS SCENE IS JUST ICONIC...

THE FUTURE...

futuristic clothes

I'M THINKING HOLOGRAMS? OR TELEPORTING? OR ROBOTS WILL DO OUR JOBS FOR US SO WE CAN DO WHAT WE WANT? WATCH THIS SPACE!

DAILY TOPICS OF CONVERSATION

MOANING ABOUT OUR QUARTER-LIFE CRISES / SHIT JOBS

BOY DRAMAS

SCREEN-SHOTS DECIPHERING MESSAGES

PLANNING ADVENTURES

MEMES (USUALLY RUPAUL / MEAN GIRLS)

TALKING & REMINISCING ABOUT HOW GREAT WE ARE

'SHOULD I BUY THIS?'

CUTE 'DOGS IN OUTFITS' PICS

YOUR CHAT MAY LOOK SOMETHING LIKE THIS. OR NOTHING LIKE THIS. YOU DO YOU.

CHAT PERSONAS

HELP!

THE NEEDY ONE

SO THE PLAN IS...

ORGANIZER

MEME QUEEN

IT'S NOT MEANT TO BEN

TYPO HO

YOU NEED TO TALK TO HIM

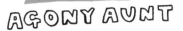

AGONY AUNT

...

SLOW-COACH REPLIER

WHAT ARE YOUR BREASTS CALLED?

(AN INVENTION FOR THOSE WITH
NICKNAME CREATIVE BLOCK)

FIRST LETTER OF FIRST NAME

A - BIG
B - SOFT
C - BOUNCY
D - POINTY
E - WOBBLY
F - SWOLLEN
G - HIGH
H - PERKY
I - SAGGY
J - HOT
K - TRIANGULAR
L - PILLOWY
M - MILKING
N - SWEATY
O - SQUISHY
P - FLAT
Q - UNUSUAL
R - SEXY
S - ATHLETIC
T - BIG NIPPED
U - FIERCE
V - ASYMMETRIC
W - JOGGING
X - OLD
Y - DANCING
Z - MODEST

FIRST LETTER OF SURNAME

A - FLYERS
B - MELONS
C - JUGS
D - LLAMAS
E - CONES
F - CUSHIONS
G - SPACE HOPPERS
H - CHESTICLES
I - PUPPIES
J - SPEED BUMPS
K - BEACH BALLS
L - HUBBA BUBBAS
M - MACHINES
N - CANS
O - GURLS
P - BAPS
Q - GLOBES
R - KNOCKERS
S - BAZOOMAS
T - WHALES
U - WHOPPERS
V - COCONUTS
W - TWINS
X - UDDERS
Y - BANGERS
Z - CHEBS

2. THOU SHALL ALL HAVE RIDICULOUS NICKNAMES

THERE'S A SMELLY MAN ON THE TRAIN

JUST ORDERED PIZZA

NOW I'M WAITING FOR THE BUS

THE DOG JUST FARTED

DRINKING GIN ON A TUESDAY

IT'S RAINING. LOTS.

3. THOU SHALL SHARE ALL UNNECESSARY DETAILS OF DAY-TO-DAY LIFE

4. NEVER MUTE THE CHAT

WHETHER IT'S BEEN
BOOKED FOR MONTHS
OR DAYS, SUMMER OR WINTER,
YOUR FIRST OR HUNDREDTH
HOLIDAY TOGETHER, YOU'RE BURSTING
WITH EXCITEMENT. AND WITH GOOD
REASON! SQUADVENTURES ARE
THE STUFF OF LEGEND...

PLACES WE'VE BEEN

PLACES LEFT TO GO

Holiday special

FORGET THEIR PANTIES

GET ON THE WRONG PLANE

HAVE A HOLIDAY ROMANCE

GET INJURED

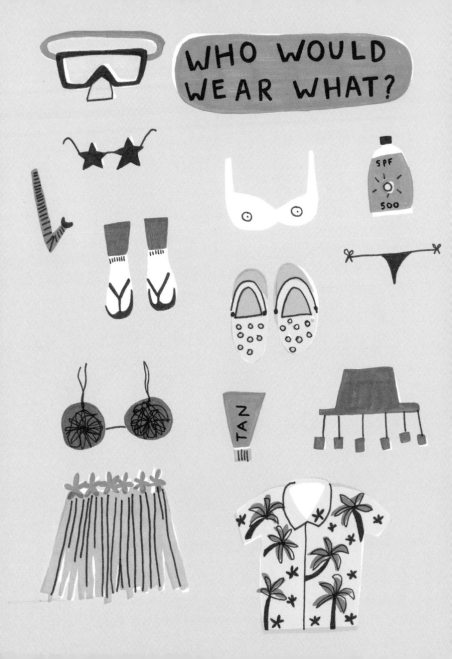

IF YOU WERE EACH A COCKTAIL, WHO WOULD BE WHAT?

MOJITO

ESPRESSO MARTINI

BLOODY MARY

PINA COLADA

LONG ISLAND ICED TEA

TEQUILA SUNRISE

STRAWBERRY DAIQUIRI

SANGRIA

SEX ON THE BEACH

WHEREVER YOU
GO AND
WHATEVER
FLOATS YOUR
BOAT, IT'S
GONNA BE
SQUAD
GOALS.

IN FACT YOU'RE SO GREAT,
SOMEONE SHOULD MAKE A
BOOK ABOUT YOU...

THE END

Gallery

THE SQUAD IS A WORK OF ART, SO USE THIS PAGE TO DOODLE EACH OTHER AS CREATIVE MASTERPIECES...

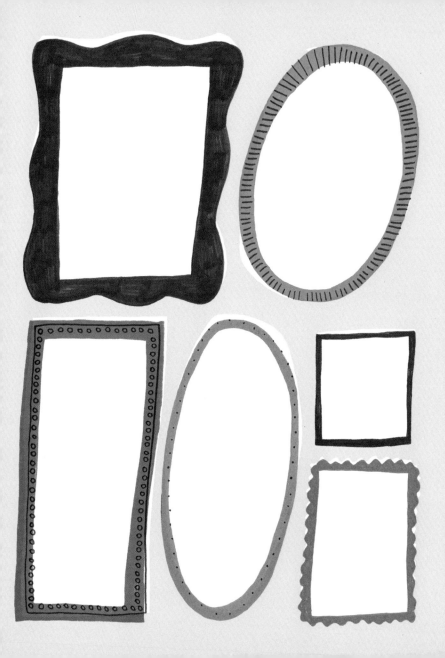

MEET THE AUTHOR

Hiya

IF I WERE A COCKTAIL,

I'D BE A SEX ON THE BEACH BECAUSE THEY'RE SWEET, STRONGER THAN YOU THINK & INAPPROPRIATE.

MY GIRL SQUAD CALL OURSELVES **CHEESE PIE.** WE ALL STUDIED ILLUSTRATION TOGETHER IN BEAUTIFUL FALMOUTH, UK.

WHEN I WAS SEVEN, I WANTED TO BE EITHER A WRITER OR A WEATHER FORECASTER.

WHEN I'M NOT DOODLING, I'M

PROBABLY CROCHETING. MY MOST SUCCESSFUL PROJECTS HAVE BEEN BEANS ON TOAST, BUNTING & A PENCIL SCARF.

I WOULD BE **GINGER SPICE** BECAUSE OF SOME INTERESTING HAIR-DYING INCIDENTS.

I WATCHED EVERY EPISODE OF F·R·I·E·N·D·S WHILE WRITING THIS BOOK. I AM 80% PHOEBE.